WALKING INTO THE NEXT CHAPTER

Your Past Will Make Your
Present More Powerful

DANA ROSE

WESTBOW
P R E S S®
A DIVISION OF THOMAS NELSON
& ZONDERVAN

WestBow Press books may be ordered through booksellers or by contacting:

WestBow Press
A Division of Thomas Nelson & Zondervan
1663 Liberty Drive
Bloomington, IN 47403
www.westbowpress.com
844-714-3454

ISBN: 979-8-3850-1085-1 (sc)
ISBN: 979-8-3850-1084-4 (e)

Library of Congress Control Number: 2023920542

Print information available on the last page.

WestBow Press rev. date: 11/07/2023

ACKNOWLEDGMENTS

Thank you to my amazing husband Arthur S. Rose for inspiring me to always pursue my dreams and aspirations. He encouraged me to continue to achieve many goals despite life's adversities. When I faced a big obstacle, he told me that through Christ I could overcome it.

CHAPTER 1

RESET AFTER TRAUMA

The beginning of a new chapter is ultimately the decision to start life afresh. It is the meaning you attach to an event that enables you to see the event as something that changes you or opens a new door in your life.

The Healing Power of Writing

Writing about your thoughts and feelings after losing someone gives you a chance to express yourself, which is rare in this highly judgmental world. It also gives you the tools to explore and discover within yourself so you can rebuild your inner strength. Do not give up! Stick to your beliefs. You have to keep going even though the path may seem strange or even dangerous at times. God will go before you, straighten the crooked places, and remove dangerous obstacles from your path. "Be steadfast in My trust that I will perfect the things that concern you," the Lord says. "I will go before you and level the mountains; I will shatter the doors of bronze and cut through the bars of iron" (Isaiah 45:2).

Beloved, don't look back. The past is behind you, and your future awaits you. Seize every moment as it comes and lean on God for strength, courage, and wisdom. You are not alone facing the world alone because He is with you whether you recognize His presence or not. The Lord will supernaturally empower you to stand up and move forward in His strength and power. The angel gave Zerubbabel this message from the Lord, "Not by might, nor by power, but by My Spirit [of whom the oil is a symbol], says the Lord of hosts" (Zechariah 4:6).

Death is a cruel and merciless enemy. We all face death at some point in our lives. You may have received bad news from your doctor. Or maybe you're struggling to move forward after the death of a son, daughter, or spouse.

Allow the Feelings

Coping with the loss of a loved one can bring up just about every emotion imaginable. Sometimes you can feel like you're losing your mind when more than one emotion seems to be prevailing at the same time. It's natural to feel this way because it's normal to experience a range of different feelings. In times of death and grief, gently remind yourself that your feelings are your own and that they are within the norm. Knowing that there is no right or wrong way to feel about the loss of a loved one is important to your process. However, God's assurance will protect and guide you.

That's what death is. It keeps surprising us; it keeps interrupting our lives. We pause to mourn. Grief hurts; it doesn't even feel right. It feels bad—so bad we want to avoid it. Our American culture doesn't *handle* death and grief very well. We avoid it, we don't talk about it, and unlike many other cultures around the world, we don't know what a *good death* is. The truth is more than half of us are actively grieving someone or suffering from a loss right now. You go out in the company of mourners. As much as we don't like it, grief is a normal life experience. This is human nature, expected and inevitable. It's not sinful. We know this because Jesus grieved.

The Grief of Jesus

When it comes to our own human experience of grief, there is no better place to look than the human experience of the Son of God mentioned by Isaiah. "A Man of sorrows and pain and acquainted with grief" (Isaiah 53:3). This is part of what it means to be human after the Fall, which means we will be "acquainted with sorrow."

Our Lord was here on earth for a little over thirty years and had only three years of active ministry. However, He did not hesitate to spend some time in grief. He made time for mourning: those moments when He wept for Lazarus, those moments when He wept and prayed in Gethsemane, and those moments when He prayed lamentations on the cross. He was even willing to spend a moment of His short but precious life mourning the hardness of the heart.

My biggest battles come when my emotions get destroyed. My dad faced a hopeless battle with a plethora of illnesses. Slowly, he went from a great man to a fragile and broken man. His death left me feeling empty, scared, and miserable!

When I think about the times in my life when I've taken quite an emotional beating, I really see how powerful God is. The enemy has done everything to bring you down, but it's not over yet. In the next chapter, your faith triumphs; truth triumphs over every lie. Let your heart be strengthened in the plan of victory over the devil. The Lord said that as long as you maintain faith and an eternal perspective, you will continue to prevail. Push through! "The Lord will go forth like a warrior, He will stir up His zeal like a man of war; He will shout out, yes, He will raise a war cry. He will prevail [mightily] against His enemies" (Isaiah 42:13).

I am entering a time of change where things will never be the same again. This is the beginning of a new era in my life; how can I start over? I use the lessons of the past as a guide on my journey. But my emotion is a spiritual calling. It will tug at your heart and become your desire to know God and serve Him. It will override all other voices or desires. You will not be able to follow Him fully unless you answer His calling. The Bible says, "For many are called [invited, summoned], but few are chosen" (Matthew 22:14).

This test in my life will determine if I will get frustrated with the process, which will make things worse, or if I will trust God to give me the wisdom I need to survive emotionally. "Peace I leave with you; My [perfect] peace I give to you; not as the world gives do I give to you. Do not let your heart be troubled, nor let it be afraid. [Let My perfect peace calm you in every circumstance and give you courage and strength for every challenge.]" (John 14:27).

God's peace gave me a chance to regroup. The fighting was intense, and my fighting took a lot of energy both mentally and physically. I had to stop in a crisis and consider where I was and where I could regain perspective. God said to draw close to Him for He would be my place of strength and safety in times of trouble. "The Lord is my rock, my fortress, and the One who rescues me; My God, my rock and strength in whom I trust and take refuge; My shield, and the horn of my salvation, my high tower—my stronghold" (Psalm 18:2).

I speak to those facing a crisis of faith. It's not that you don't believe in a higher power or take my word for it. It's your symptoms that speak louder than your beliefs. Pause and remember that God can heal you. Nothing is too difficult for God. Be firm in your resolve to truly believe in total healing. "Be strong and unshakable," said the Lord. "Then they cried out to the Lord in their trouble, And He saved them from their distresses. He sent His word and healed them, And rescued them from their destruction. Let them give thanks to the Lord for His lovingkindness, And for His wonderful acts to the children of men! And let them offer the sacrifices of thanksgiving, And speak of His deeds with shouts of joy!" (Psalm 107:19–22).

When I'm trying to stay focused, my mind wanders from relevant matters to recalling the past to convey a sense of failure and judgment. Don't dwell on the past or let regret hold you back from walking in the Spirit. "Get rid of torment," says the Lord, "and be free." Galatians 5:1 says, "It was for this freedom that Christ set us free [completely liberating us]; therefore keep standing firm and do not be subject again to a yoke of slavery [which you once removed]."

I refuse to let the enemy judge things that are beyond my control. The Lord said to me that in these times my faith must be firmly attached to the fact that I have nothing impossible for God to solve. Trust God to share your burden. "Come to Me, all who are weary and heavily burdened [by religious rituals that provide no peace], and I will give you rest [refreshing your souls with salvation]. Take My yoke upon you and learn from Me [following Me as My disciple], for I am gentle and humble in heart, and you will find rest [renewal, blessed quiet] for your souls. For My yoke is easy [to bear] and My burden is light" (Matthew 11:28–30).

Let faith rule in every situation. Refuse to allow fear to have any locus of control. Hold on to what you know, and God will hear your prayers and answer when you call. He will give divine guidance to spiritual perfection. "You will see my glory and be amazed," said the Lord. "I am your stronghold, your tower, and safe haven. I am your rock!" "Yes, You are my rock and my fortress; For Your name's sake You will lead me and guide me" (Psalm 31:3).

CHAPTER 2

ABOUT MY STORY

I have been through so much trauma during a vulnerable time in my life. For as long as I can remember, I've shared my personal stories based on facts. Most importantly, I take back my right to preserve my own legacy, my identity, and my true essence as a woman for the record. I sincerely believe that I am waging a spiritual battle during this deep, dark time in my life. Only the grace of God has brought me victory. God guides me by grace and mercy to live the life I deserve on the path I started. Every day of our lives tells a story, but they also help others tell their stories. Writing and documenting my life story has been very helpful on my journey so I can take advantage of what I've learned along the way. It doesn't just affect other people. This is also an advantage for you. This way we can fully understand the dynamic impact of our history on our future.

I made my own documentary on teaching others how to move forward in times of pain and uncertainty. I realized trauma had affected my life so much that I didn't want the pain to affect my future. In contrast, many people who experience traumatic events advocate positive outcomes, such as new perspectives on life, spiritual renewal, and personal growth. As I started to move toward the goal of "the darkness didn't stop me," I had to ask myself a few questions that were important to extracting my story: (1) Who are you? (2) Where were you born? (3) Where do you put your fear and trauma? (4) Where is your academic path headed? and (5) How do you do more than one thing at a time? My goal is not to have an inspiring story. The goal is to be able to use my story as a weapon! It is a guide for those who want to overcome obstacles. "The weapons of our warfare are not physical [weapons of flesh and blood]. Our weapons are divinely powerful for the destruction of fortresses" (2 Corinthians 10:4).

Once we have mastered our mental state of mind, we move to generosity. In this shift, don't abdicate your responsibility to record history. You document your state. Remember, your legacy is not the end of your life. This is the end of a level. We must never forget how important it is to remember how you did it! There is strength in our

Being nosy, one day Clover and Naida spotted Arielle going in and out of the building. "This doesn't look very promising, Naida, if Arielle has anything to do with it. We need to overhear some of the conversations between the men and Ginger."

Clover and Naida began staying closer to the building and out of sight to overhear conversations. Surprisingly one day it wasn't Ginger at the site, it was Arielle giving the orders. Naida bends over to Clover and whispers. "It's a house for Arielle."

"Drats! This can't be. She doesn't deserve a house. She's mean, she's cruel, and she's immoral," screamed Clover." She stamped her feet and turned red in the face with anger and flew around furiously.

"What shall we do, Clover?" asked Naida.

"I don't know, but I'll think of something soon. She has to be stopped."

The following night, Clover flew to Naida's house. "Come on Naida, I have an idea."

Naida followed Clover to Arielle's new home. "What are we doing, Clover?"

"Help me haul the water hose over to the window."

Naida realizes what Clover is up to. After much struggling, they get it to a window and slipped it inside the house.

"Turn it on, Naida."

When the workers arrive the next morning, everything is soaked and ruined. Ginger was called out to the house by the contractor.

"Oh my goodness, who would do a mean thing like this?" asked Ginger.

"I don't know madam but there must be somebody that has a grudge against someone," said the contractor.

"Go ahead and replace and repair what needs to be done and I'll talk to Arielle. When Ginger told Arielle, she became furious. She knew who did it and now she's going to have to take steps to make sure it doesn't happen again.

Arielle went to work again looking for a large spider web among the trees in the forest. When she found one, she lifted it carefully from the tree and left to find Naida. She spotted her alone and unsuspecting.

"Well, Naida, it looks as though you and your friend are looking for trouble. Guess what? I've got good news for you; you've just found it!" Arielle threw the web over Naida.

"Stop it Arielle, let me go! You're not going to get away with this."

"And who's going to stop me, Naida, your best friend, Clover? She can't stop an ant from climbing onto an elephant's behind. Now, let's find a nice hideout for you. Where would you like to be, Naida?"

"Arielle, this isn't funny."

"Oh, I know it's not, Naida. How well I know it. It wasn't funny when you and Clover ran the water into my new house either was it? Well, maybe it was funny for the two of you, but now you're going to pay."

"We didn't do it, Arielle."

"Whoa, Naida, I don't believe a word you say. What happens when you lie, Naida? Your nose might start growing long like Pinocchio's. Gosh, you're getting heavy, you must weigh a hundred pounds soaking wet,"

"You re not funny at all, Arielle. You just wait," cried Naida.

"Wait? Wait for what? For you and Clover to do more damage? I don't think so. Oh look, Naida. There's a very tall oak. Isn't it beautiful with all the moss hanging from it? Perfect! It's perfect for your new home."

"No, Arielle! No! Don't do this to me."

"That's funny, I could have said the same thing to you and Clover when you put the hose and ran water into my house if I had been there but I wasn't, was I?" Arielle flew to the tip-top of the tree and wrapped the web around one of the branches. She covered Naida completely with the web except for her face then placed moss around her.

"I'm going to get even with you, Arielle."

"We'll see. I'll be back, Naida, don't go away."

Arielle snickered and flew away in search of another spider web.

After she found one, she looked for Clover. When she spotted her she swooped down and KABLAMM the web covered her.

"Hey, stop it!" screamed Clover.

"Hi Clover! Surprise! Surprise! What a nosy little busy body, snooping around my place. Did you just want to make sure you ruined it? You've gone too far Clover."

"Arielle, I haven't done anything to you yet," cried clover.

"You think not? You lie and were were looking for trouble and you've just found it; the same as your friend, Naida."

Arielle flew to a distant village and spotted a tall tree. She placed the web over a branch then pulled the web away from Clover's face so she could breathe and be fed. Once Arielle finished getting Clover settled, she flew back home and went to see Magic.

"Magic, we've gotten Clover and Naida out of the way for a while so I think we'll go back to our money-making job before Queen Rhiannon returns. We still need to buy furniture for our new home. We can destroy good deeds another time."

"Destroy deeds another time, yes," said Magic.

Two or three times daily Arielle faithfully took food and water to Clover and Naida. She hadn't put them out to die; she wanted to teach them a lesson. When she took food to Clover the next day, Clover was angry. "You may as well let me die, Arielle, it would be more kind. I haven't done anything to you."

"I could not do that Clover. You have not done anything so wicked that you deserve to die. Hmpff, it seems I've heard that line before. I wonder where I heard it. Oh, yes, now I remember. It was about the time that big old nasty spider was just about to eat you for dinner. Remember that Clover?"

"I'll do anything to help you, Arielle; just don't leave me here by myself, please."

Arielle wasn't listening. She was mad and she wanted to get even.

"I'll be back, Clover, I promise. Ta-ta!" said Arielle and flew to Ginger's house.

"Hi, Arielle, what have you been up to?" asked Ginger.

"Oh, I just finished hanging out some dirty laundry. Are the workers repairing the damage?"

"Oh, yes, they'll be finished in a couple of days then they'll get on with the construction."

"Good. I'll go by and check it out. Thanks, Ginger."

Arielle flew by the building site, inspected it and then went home.

"Welcome home, Master! I miss you," said Magic.

"How's my favorite boy? Well, the builders are coming along nicely with our home, Magic. Soon we won't have to live in a crummy old tree and you'll have a nice large home of your own."

"Sounds good, Master, but too big for Magic?"

"Oh, no, Magic. Come spring I'm going to catch a mate for you."

"You kid Magic?"

Arielle giggled. "No, no, I'm not kidding."

"Yippee! A lady, a lady!" squawked Magic as he jumped up and down and flew around and around doing flips.

"Why, Magic, I didn't know you were so wild about ladies."

"Magic wild, wild, wild about ladies. Can't wait, can't wait."

A month later Arielle's home was finished and Ginger moved into the house on the third floor. She planted flowers, shrubs and many trees on the grounds and the rooftop. Arielle helped as much as she could then went to the aviary.

When Magic heard her enter, he looked at her with bright eyes. "Hi, Master!"

"Magic, tomorrow we can go into some villages and destroy all the good deeds that our Fairy Godmothers have done. Then I can become the villager's ruler."

"If that is your wish, Master," said Magic as he lowered his head.

"Yes, it is, and then I'll have people looking up to me and admiring me."

Meanwhile in the villages, the townspeople were hearing mournful cries every night. They didn't know where they were coming from or why it was happening. The cries were leaving them depressed, unhappy, lonely, and angry.

The following night, Arielle entered Magic's aviary. "Hi Master. We go tonight?"

"Yes, Magic, we are."

Late that night Arielle flew into the aviary and onto Magic's back and they flew off. On the way out, Arielle began her chant.

"Fireflies of the night; come with me on my plight; grip the deeds of kind tonight; and take them to a troglodyte. Oh, whatever, just take them away," said Arielle.

The fireflies followed Magic by the hundreds into the nearest village and collected all the good deeds. They continued on to all the villages until all the deeds had been abandoned.

When they finished, Magic asked; "Home Master?"

"Yes, Magic, our job is done for now. We are going to take a break." But before Arielle was ready to announce that she would be the ruler of the fairies, the villagers were still in an uproar.

A few weeks had passed. Arielle entered the aviary one day to see Magic.

"Master, I feel tense."

"Why is that, Magic?"

"Not sure, like something wrong."

"Okay, Magic, we'll go release Clover and Naida tomorrow and see if that will help you feel better."

The following morning Arielle and Magic flew to Beaver Falls and released Naida from her web and headed towards Bay Village to release Clover.

"Where Clover, Master?"

"Go to the majestic oak with the beautiful moss," said Arielle.

"Where?" asked Magic again.

"She's inside the big clump of moss over there," as she pointed to the oak. Magic flew to the clump of moss.

When Clover saw her, she asked; "What do you want now, Arielle?"

"I have come to release you Clover. You are free to go home. I have released Naida too."

"Well don't ask me for a pat on the back because it will be a long time coming, Arielle. One day you will be a victim of your own greed," said Clover.

"I don't expect anything from you or Naida other than staying out of my business."

"Hmpff," said Clover and flew off to find her friend, Naida.

Magic and Arielle flew back home. When they arrived, Arielle flew into his cage and fluttered down from his back. "I hope you will feel better now Magic. Next week is the Annual Starling Hunt and I will find a mate for you."

"Goodie, goodie, can't wait. I happy, I happy."

Arielle smiled and shut the cage door. She busied herself in her garden all week while waiting for the Starling Hunt. When the time came, she flew to the swamp and danced on the wild flowers while singing while waiting for Queen Rhiannon. She looked across the swamp and saw the same male fairy she had seen before staring at her.

I've seen him before, she thought. Why can't I remember where?

When she heard Queen Rhiannon arrive, she flew over to the rest of the group.

All eyes were on the queen when she spoke. "You all know why we are here this morning. For those of you who weren't able to catch a starling last year, I wish you good luck today. They will be roosting on the west side of the forest. Remember to obey the rules if you catch one this year. Thanks for coming, you are free to go."

"Queen Rhiannon, I wish to catch one. I...said Naida, faltering after she looked over and saw Arielle with a mean look on her face; so she said nothing more.

When the fairies left, a cloud of silvery dust filled the air again. Arielle flew in the opposite direction as usual, hunting for a large spider web. After she found the one she liked, she looked for a female starling.

. When she spotted one, she plunked the web over the first female she saw. "Aha! Gotcha, she cried out. Magic is going to be so happy. '

"Caw, caw, caw," cried the bird.

"Calm down, you will have a new boyfriend in a matter of

minutes. He will even teach you to talk. My, what a Lucky Lady you are going to be. Whoa, that's a nice name. That is what we'll call you, "Lucky Lady."

Arielle wrapped the cobweb around her carefully and carried her home to Magic. When she opened the door to the aviary, she set her down and removed the cobweb.

Magic was so excited he flew around calling out, "pretty lady, pretty lady. She nice, she nice," he said excitedly.

Arielle laughed at him because he was being so giddy. "I thought you'd like her Magic. Her name is Lucky Lady. Do you like the name?"

"Yes, yes, pretty Lucky Lady."

"Good, I'm happy for you Magic. I'll have to find a nesting box. I'm sure we'll have little ones flying around in no time."

"Yes, yes, little ones, Lucky Lady."

Arielle laughed, turned and went into the house to see Ginger.

"Ginger, you'll have to go out and meet Lucky Lady. I caught her today and brought her home to Magic. He fell in love with her instantly."

"Sure, that's great. I'll go out to meet her. I've been working in your garden. It's beginning to look awesome, Arielle. You're going to love it when everything has grown taller. Go up and take a look at it."

"All right, I'll go now. I'm anxious to see it. That will be my home; my home on top of the world," said Arielle.

Arielle flew up to the top of her mansion. Her face ignited like a light bulb. Ginger had planted beautiful flowers with a lot of bluebells and shrubs. She looked over near the bluebells and spotted a machine. There was an elegant bench just her size sitting by the bluebells. She flew back to Ginger.

"Well, do you like it?" asked Ginger.

"Like it? No, Ginger I love it."

She flew up and kissed Ginger on the cheek. "Why thank you Arielle. That's very sweet of you."

"Not everyone thinks I'm sweet. What is the machine for, Ginger?"

"That's a special surprise for you. When you dance, just push the button on the top."

"Oh, okay," said Arielle "Thank you."

Ginger smiled at Arielle and shook her head. She wasn't aware of Arielle's unkind dealings that she had been up to with the townspeople.

Ginger went to the aviary to meet Lucky Lady. "Well, Magic, what a beautiful lady you have there," said Ginger.

"Yes, Ginger, Lucky Lady."

"She certainly is, Magic, very lucky, indeed. I hope the two of you are very happy together."

"Yes, very happy," said Magic.

Ginger left them and went back into the house.

After a few weeks had passed, and Arielle had left Magic alone with his new mate so they could get acquainted; she went to see Ginger to ask a favor of her.

"Ginger, will you go to a pet shop and purchase a nesting box for Lucky Lady? When the time comes, she's going to need one."

"Sure, I'll pick one up and mount it in the aviary."

"Thanks," said Arielle and she flew to the roof of her mansion to enjoy the scenery around her.

Later in the week, Ginger purchased a nesting box for the aviary and a small fairy house to place under shrubbery in the backyard for Arielle if she ever wanted to use it.

After ten days had passed, Arielle approached Ginger. "I think Lucky Lady is setting, I don't know how long it takes but I think we'll be seeing babies before long."

"Really?" asked Ginger.

"Yes, when I fed this morning she was still in the nesting box," said Arielle.

"How great. We will have little ones flying about soon. That will be so exciting. I'm sure Magic will be a proud father and a very good one too. Have you heard Lucky Lady say any words yet?" asked Ginger.

"No, but I don't spend a lot of time in the aviary anymore. I don't want to interfere with their life."

The villagers of Beaver Falls have not heard the mourning for a long time but they are still unhappy and fighting in the streets throwing sticks and stones at each other without knowing why.

In the next few days, Lucky Lady's eggs have hatched.

Magic was so excited he flew about shouting; "Oh boy, oh boy, new babies, new babies," he cried.

"Yes, Magic, we are proud parents of new babies," said Lucky Lady.

Magic looked at Lucky Lady with a surprised look, "You talk now?" he asked.

"Yes, I know little, thanks to you and Ginger, Magic."

Magic flew around excitedly doing flips and yelling out. 'Babies, babies, babies!" cries Magic.

Arielle heard him screaming from above. She flew down to the aviary to see what was going on.

"Babies, Master, babies."

"Wonderful, Magic. How many?"

"I think seven. How many, Lucky Lady?" asked Magic.

"Seven," said Lucky Lady.

"Why Magic, you've taught Lucky Lady to talk," said Arielle.

"Some, Master, some."

"I'm so happy for you both, Magic."

"Yes, happy, Magic happy too."

Queen Rhiannon has arrived back in the forest. She received word that the villages are in an uproar. Immediately, she called a mandatory meeting for all the fairies under Old Noble.

"I am not a happy Queen. I have been forsaken, ridiculed and abandoned by one of our own. One of you have disobeyed our covenants and bargained with the devil. I'm here to tell you, to bargain with the devil is no bargain at all. The villagers are rioting due to stress and uneasiness. I demand the guilty party step forward and face the consequences. A hush fell over the crowd. As Arielle listened to the Queen, she knew who she was talking about. She also knew who the snitches were. She appeared to be calm on the outside but was seething on the inside.

Alvin, a noble friend of the people, a male fairy offered Queen Rhiannon his service.

"Your Highness, may I offer my services?" asked Alvin.

"And what might your services be, young man?" asked Queen Rhiannon.

"I am Alvin, a servant of the people, Your Highness. I can find the party that is to blame but I believe that whoever it may be is innocent until proven guilty. I think it is just someone that's chasing rainbows in the night."

Arielle looked at Alvin and raised her eyebrows wondering what this guy is up to. Is he some kind of wacko, or what? She has seen him before, but where and when? Why can't she remember?

"All right Alvin, report to me as soon as you find something. This sort of behavior is not acceptable. It presents a bleak picture for our future of survival as good fairies," said Queen Rhiannon.

"Yes, Your Highness, as soon as I can get a firm grasp on any information," said Alvin.

The meeting adjourned and everyone left. Arielle went home and into the aviary.

"Hi, Magic," said Arielle downheartedly.

"Something wrong, Master?"

"I don't know. Just feeling blue I guess. The queen called a meeting and I think she knows something. She has some guy investigating why the people of the villages are unhappy."

"Maybe best to tell truth, Master."

"This guy, Alvin, told the queen he thought someone was chasing rainbows in the night. What does that mean, Magic?"

"It means there are no rainbows at night so you won't find any pot of gold or whatever it is you're looking for."

"Hmmm, I already have what I was looking for, but then he told the queen when he gets a grasp on something, he'll let her know."

"Know what, Master?"

"I don't know, but if he thinks he's going to grasp any part of me, I'll fly him to the moon in a cocoon."

Magic roared with laughter. "I'd say that's taking him a little too serious, Master."

"Well, I think he's an oddball, besides I don't like men, well, except you Magic," said Arielle smiling.

"I'm happy for that, Master."

As Arielle talked, she suddenly remembered where she had seen Alvin.

"Magic! I remember where I've seen him; and more than one time. Oh yes, it was Alvin. I've seen him staring at me more than once in the swamp while I was dancing on flowers. 'Alvin,' that's a funny name for a man. It makes me think of Alvin and the Chipmunks, but he certainly doesn't look like a chipmunk. He is actually quite handsome."

"At least you remembered, Master."

"How are the babies doing, Magic?"

"Fine, Master, fine. Growing like hotcakes!"

Arielle lets out a peal of laughter. "Thanks for making me feel better, Magic."

Arielle flew back up to her penthouse. Maybe if she dances, she'll feel better. She thought of the machine by the bluebells. She flew over and pounced on the button and bubbles float up in every color of the rainbow. "Oh my goodness, they're so beautiful." While she was dancing, Ginger started yelling.

Arielle heard Ginger's cries of distress so she flew back to see what was wrong. The garbage can was on fire in the back yard. "Quick, get the water hose, Ginger!" cried Arielle.

By the time Ginger got the hose hooked up and the water turned on, the fire had jumped to a nearby tree, then another and another. Soon the forest was on fire.

"Help, Arielle, do something! I can't get it under control. It's spreading too fast and the hose isn't large or long enough to put it out," screamed Ginger.

"Go call the fire department, Ginger, before it gets to the house, hurry! I will keep trying to put it out."

Ginger dropped the hose and ran to the house. Soon the fire department was there and put the fire out.

"l wonder how the fire got started, Arielle." said Ginger while still shaking from the ordeal.

"I'm not sure, but I think I know who it was," said Arielle.

That's all she wanted Ginger to know. Ginger looked toward the house and saw bubbles soaring into the sky.

"Oh, you found what the machine does, Arielle?"

"Yes Ginger, they're so beautiful. I was dancing when you called out. Thank you for the machine Ginger and for being such a kind friend. I'd better go up and turn it off."

"Your welcome, Arielle, I love to see you happy."

Arielle flew up to the penthouse to turn the machine off and walked in front of it. When she did, a bubble formed around her. She smiled and looked around as she spiraled upward.

"Ginger, Ginger, look up, look at me!" yelled Arielle.

Arielle looked out over the world around her. She spotted Alvin staring up at her and saw Ginger waving from the ground. When the bubble burst, Arielle flew down onto Ginger's shoulder laughing.

"Gee, I wish I could do that, Arielle. That looked so fun and exciting."

"It was breath-taking, Ginger. I want to do that more often. I could see the world. Oh, thank you, Ginger, thank you for the bubble machine. I love it and I love you."

"You're sure welcome, Arielle, I'm glad it makes you happy." said Ginger smiling.

"Oh it does, but you know what Ginger?"

"What?"

"I saw Alvin out there staring up at me again. He's beginning to freak me out. I don't know what he's up to."

"You'll find out in time, don't let him get to you, Arielle. He's harmless, I'm sure."

"I hope so but I'm not so sure that he's not the one causing some of the problems."

Arielle flew back to her penthouse and turned the bubble machine off before she stood in front of it again. She sat down on her bench and thought about the villages. Soon she'll go there with Magic and start making friends with the people to try to calm their fears. She thought she'd better forget about becoming their ruler. She has already done enough harm but she has done what she set out to do; have a new home. She will give the babies more time to grow and learn to fly and eat on their own.

In the following days, Arielle spent her time in the aviary with Magic, Lucky Lady and the babies. They are out of the nest now and flying around in the aviary.

"What do you think, Master?" asked Magic.

"About what?"

"The babies."

"They are beautiful, Magic. It won't be long, and you'll be able to leave them for a while and we can go to the villages again."

"For what, Master?"

"To make friends and calm their fears."

"What do you mean asked Magic. First you are their enemy, now a friend?"

"I was never an enemy, Magic. I like people, but I didn't want to live in a rotten old tree for the rest of my life. I knew I was wrong but it was the only way for me to get ahead after a life of poverty. I guess I was getting out of hand when I started talking about being their ruler."

"Okay Master, I understand now."

The next day Arielle decided to turn the bubble machine on. The bubbles were pouring out by the hundreds in the brilliant colors of the rainbow. She started to dance and sing.

Below Alvin heard Arielle singing. The bubble machine was pouring out bubbles by the hundreds and they floated everywhere. When one came near Alvin, he hopped on and a gust of wind whirled him upward.

When the bubble reached the penthouse, Alvin jumped off and grabbed Arielle's hand and began to dance with her. Arielle stopped and stamped her feet. "What are you doing here? Get out! Get out now," she shouted.

"I heard you singing, and it sounded so angelic I had to come up to be with you. The singing and the bubbles are as beautiful as you are; even when you are mad, pretty lady."

Arielle was as mad as a wet hen, but she blushed anyway. "Why are you watching me? Are you spying on me? Are you going to tell the queen? What are you doing?" asked Arielle angrily.

"N-Nothing, you sounded so beautiful, and you are beautiful."

"You said that once before, do you stutter?" asked Arielle.

"N-No. I'll be leaving now; I'm sorry I interrupted you." Alvin flew away leaving Arielle puzzled. She flew down to see Ginger.

"Ginger, Alvin, the little creep that's been hanging around, just flew up to my penthouse and started dancing with me. He said he heard me singing from the ground and it sounded so angelic, he had to come up to enjoy it, and on a bubble at that!"

"Why, Arielle, I do believe you have a suitor."

"A suitor? What's that?"

"Someone that is trying to woo you, Arielle, he likes you."

"Likes me? Why would anyone like me?"

"You're beautiful and a beautiful person, Arielle, hasn't anyone ever told you that before?"

"No, except Alvin a few minutes ago."

"Well, believe it, Arielle you are very beautiful."

After their chat, Arielle went back to the penthouse. She sat outside on her bench wile pondering what Alvin and Ginger had told her; that she is beautiful. Tears start welling up in her eyes, and soon they were like a river flowing down her cheeks. No one had ever told her that before. No one had ever liked her enough to tell her that. Feeling sad, she went down to the aviary.

"Hi, Magic," said Arielle, sadly.

"Master, what's wrong?"

"You know that guy Alvin that I told you about?"

"Yeah? What about him?"

"When I was in my garden at the penthouse, he floated up on a bubble and jumped off wanting to dance with me. Then he told me I'm beautiful. Do you think I am beautiful, Magic?"

"Oh yes, by far, Master, you are very beautiful."

"But what about the inside of me, Magic?"

"You can use some improvement in that respect, Master."

Arielle lowered her head in shame. "I remember my mother telling me that looking beautiful is one thing but being beautiful is quite another. What does it mean Magic, and how do I change?"

"One day it will come if there is a desire to change, Master; it will just be there like a flash of light," said Magic.

"Okay, Magic. Do you think the children are old enough for us to go to the villages? I think that will be a good place for me to start."

"Give them another month, Master, and they will be on their own."

"All right Magic, thanks." Arielle walked away feeling a heavy heart. After she left Magic, she went to see Ginger again.

"Hi, Arielle," said Ginger.

"Hi."

"Is something wrong?"

"I'm just feeling awful, Ginger."

"Why?"

"Because everyone is telling me I'm beautiful, but I don't feel beautiful on the inside."

"So, what's your option?" asked Ginger.

"I want to change but I don't know how."

Ginger looked at Arielle. "Why do you feel the need to change, Arielle; is it because of Alvin?"

"Oh no, I suddenly realize that I'm not as beautiful inside as everyone says I am. I've done bad things to people and to children, Ginger."

"What could a sweet fairy like you possibly do wrong, Arielle? We all do bad things at one time or another in our lifetime; but if it is change you want, sometimes it takes years or perhaps something drastic to happen; but change can come if you believe in yourself and wish for it."

"Okay Ginger, I'll do it and I'll wish with all my heart. Now, I think I'll go and watch the flowers growing and the bubbles bubbling. Thanks for being my friend, Ginger."

"Atta girl," said Ginger.

As soon as Arielle went up to the penthouse, she pounced on the bubble machine and sat on her bench watching the bubbles and thought about Alvin as the bubbles floated through the air. He is very handsome. Is it true someone could really care about her? She brushed off the thought and watched the colorful bubbles rise in the air.

After the second week had passed, Arielle was getting bored so she approached Magic in the aviary. "Hi Magic, could you take me to the villages today," she asked.

"Of course, I need to get out. These little ones are driving me nuts."

Arielle laughed and opened the door to let him out. Once he was out, she closed it making sure it was locked securely and flew onto his back. They arrived in Beaver Falls and when she looked around and she saw angry people fighting and calling names and throwing stones.

"They don't look happy do they Master?"

"No, they don't but I plan on changing that Magic. I've decided I don't want to be a ruler, I'd much rather becomes their friend."

"That's good Master; that makes me happy."

Arielle spotted a woman working in her garden and flew to her landing on her shoulder.

"Hi, my name is Arielle, what is yours?"

The woman looked around but didn't see anyone.

"She doesn't see you, Master."

Arielle flew around in front of her face waving her arms. "Yoo hoo, I'm here, I'm here!"

"Oh my goodness, a wee little fairy, how beautiful you are," said the woman.

"Thanks, but I'm not as beautiful on the inside as I am on the outside. My name is Arielle."

"It's nice to meet you Arielle. That happens to be true with a lot of people, Arielle, but only you can change it my little friend."

"I know, and I'm trying," said Arielle.

"That's a good sign, Arielle. How do you like my garden?"

"It's beautiful, madam, but you need to plant bluebells, a lot of ferns, some tulips and foxgloves too," said Arielle.

"Why should I plant those?"

"Do you like fairies?" asked Arielle.

"Oh yes. They are a good omen," said the woman.

"Trust me; those flowers will bring the fairies."

"Really, how?"

"The fairies dance to the bluebells because of the tinkling of the bells. They sleep on the ferns and the tulip buds are used for the babies to sleep in and the foxgloves are used for their clothing."

"Are you wearing a foxglove?" asked the woman.

"Yes, madam."

"How beautiful you are, Arielle, I'll plant every one of them and I'll tell all my friends about you."

"Thank you, madam, I'll come back another day." said Arielle as she flew back to Magic.

Magic had been sitting in the tree listening to Arielle talk to the woman and unknown to Arielle, Alvin was next door giving thoughtful attention to her while helping someone else with their garden.

"You were wonderful, Master. I'm very proud of you."

"Thank you, kind sir," replied Arielle.

Arielle looked over at the lady next door and standing next to her was Alvin. Her heart started beating in a panicky rhythm and she felt herself turning red.

"Why, Miss Arielle, you're blushing," said Magic.

"Hush, Magic. I don't want anyone to hear you. And that's the first time I've heard you call me anything except Master, I like it, Magic. Please call me Miss Arielle from now on."

"All right, Miss Arielle, I like it too. It sounds very southern and very lady like. Now stop staring at Mr. Alvin, haven't you learned it's rude to stare?" asked Magic.

Arielle smiled and turned beet red knowing that she was caught in the act but she felt good about it for some unknown reason. When they got home, Ginger ran out to meet them shouting to the top of her lungs.

"They're gone, the babies are gone; someone opened the door. They're gone Arielle, they're all gone," cried Ginger.

"No, no, not my babies, they can't be gone, cried Magic as he looked around.

"Where's Lucky Lady?"

"She's gone too, they're all gone, Magic," cried Ginger. "It's my fault, it's my entire fault, I should have seen them open the door. I'm so sorry, Magic." Ginger began to cry.

"We find them Ginger, don't cry," said Magic.

Arielle's first thought was Alvin, and then she remembered she saw him at Beaver Falls. A wave of relief swept over her.

"Come on, Magic, let's go look for them." Ariclle flew onto Magic's back and they started into the forest calling Lucky Lady.

"Lucky Lady, Lucky Lady," cried Magic.

"Lucky Lady, where are you?" called out Arielle. They called until nightfall with no success.

After a few months passed, things were beginning to improve and the fact that Magic's family had disappeared was being accepted.

One day Arielle decided to go deeper into the forest. She enjoyed the beauty and the fresh smell of pine in the forest. She fluttered around happily and then caught sight of Alvin. Her heart began beating in a panicky rhythm again and she began blushing.

What is wrong with me she wondered? Why is my heart pounding and my knees feel like jello? Be still my beating heart, she thought. Could it be Alvin that is causing this feeling within myself. She flew back home to quell the thoughts she was having.

Later in the week in Bay Village while Alvin was attending a

customer's garden he heard his name being called. He looked up and saw Lucky Lady in a tree with her babies.

"You are Alvin aren't you? Do you know Arielle?" she asked.

"Yes, I am Alvin and yes I do know Arielle. Are you Lucky Lady?" he asked.

"I surely am. My children and I are lost. We have been trying to find our way back home. Would you mind showing us the way to Arielle's home where Magic is?" she asked.

"Yes, of course, I would be very pleased to. Doing so would allow us to kill two stones with one bird….oh, uh, I mean we could kill two birds with one stone. Oh, forget it; I'm flustered and very happy to show you the way back to Arielle's place. Follow me."

When they arrived at Arielle's house, Alvin, Lucky Lady and the children flew to Magic's cage and he began screeching and doing flips when he saw them. Arielle heard him from the penthouse and flew down to see what the commotion was about.

When she arrived at the aviary, Alvin addressed her. "Miss Arielle they were lost and couldn't find their way home. Lucky Lady remembered me so I brought her and the babies back.

Arielle was stunned, shocked, speechless and a blush red. "Oh, Alvin, I'm so sorry I treated you so poorly. Can you forgive me?" she asked.

"Yes, Miss Arielle, I certainly can. All I ask in return is a date with you."

"Oh, why, why, oh my goodness, I-I guess so, it's the least I can do."

"You are mighty pretty when you a such a rosy pink, Miss Arielle."

"Thank you," she said and turned a passionate red. She jokingly pulled out her magic wand from her pocket and when she did, Alvin made a quick spin and stood before her in a black magic cloak. Arielle's mouth flew open. "Mr. Alvin, I didn't know you had it in you," she said.

Alvin laughed. "There are a lot of things you don't know about me Miss Arielle. Would you like to learn more?"

"Y-Yes, I would Mr. Alvin, very much so," said Arielle. She found herself falling for Alvin. She had never felt this way before.

Arielle's heart was in her throat. She was feeling giddy. She wanted to change her ways and she was anxious to start working on it. she went to see Magic.

Later in the day she went to see Magic.

"Magic will you take me to Beaver Falls today,' Arielle asked.

"Sure, Miss Arielle, I'd be pleased to go with you."

Arielle was planning on helping the ladies with their gardening and promoting more flowers for the fairies. During their flight, Arielle asked Magic a question. "What do you think of Alvin, Magic?"

"He a good looking man."

Arielle giggled. "No silly, I mean as a person."

"A fine man. Good catch Miss Arielle."

"Magic! Are you trying to get me married off?"

"Well, not bad idea, Miss Arielle," said Magic.

Arielle smiled and started blushing at the thought. When they reached Beaver Falls, there was a riot in the streets. A large stone hit Magic in the head and he went down with Arielle still on top of him. She jumped off and ran to him and cradled his head in her arms.

"Magic! Magic! No, no, don't leave me Magic. Please Magic; oh no, what have I done? What have I done Magic? I'm so sorry. Please don't leave me," cried Arielle. Magic lay still. Arielle sobbed uncontrollably. She stayed with him; not wanting to leave when someone came and took her by the arm.

"Come, Miss Arielle, He's gone, Magic is gone," said Alvin. Arielle is sobbing relentlessly. He took her into his arms and held her tight. I'm so sorry Miss Arielle he whispered.

Alvin was so in love with her; but he had to find out if she was the thief in the night as he suspected. Now, since he is in love with her, he knows he must protect her against all odds. This isn't the right time to ask he told himself but it had to be done. He had to know. "It was you and Magic wasn't it Miss Arielle?" he asked.

She looked up at him. "Wh-What?" she cried with stinging tears flowing down her cheeks.

"You were taking from the children, weren't you?" He took his handkerchief and wiped away her tears.

"I didn't mean to kill him. If I could take it all back, I would. I didn't want him to die," sobbed Arielle.

"Yes, I know, Miss Arielle. No one will ever know but I want you to understand; it wasn't you that killed him."

Arielle rested her head on Alvin's shoulder with tears still gently flowing down her cheeks. She looked up into his eyes and saw goodness, understanding and strength through her tears.

"Come, I'll take you home." He lifted her gently by the arm and took her back to the penthouse. He laid her on the couch and flew down to Ginger and told her of Magic's passing and asked for a cold pack. He stayed and cared for her the rest of the night while lovingly rubbing cold packs over her face. After many hours of distress, Arielle fell into a fitful sleep. When she awoke the next morning, Alvin was still there.

"Didn't you go home, Alvin? Have you been here all night?" asked Arielle.

"Yes, I've been here all night. Arielle, I can't hold my feelings in any longer. It seems I've been following you around all my life just to get a glimpse of you. I love you from the bottom of my heart, Arielle. and I want you to be my wife."

"M-Me, Alvin? Why me?"

"Why not you? You are a good fairy and a beautiful one at that."

"Good!?" "Beautiful?"

Alvin went down on his knees and took Arielle's hand. "Will you marry me, Miss Arielle?" he asked.

"But Alvin, I just killed my best friend."

Alvin shook his head no; still on bent knees and holding her hand, he said, "Listen to me, Arielle, and I'm not going to repeat this again; you did nothing. We all have a time to go. We don't know when or where it will be but we have to go on and live our lives to the fullest and I believe Magic did just that."

"He was the only friend I ever had besides Ginger, Alvin," said Arielle while blinking back tears again.

"Yes, I know, pretty lady, but you still have Ginger, Lucky Lady and the children and now you have my love too. Will you please answer my question so I can get off my knees?" asked Alvin tenderly.

Arielle smiled. "Thanks, Alvin."

"Does that mean yes?"

Arielle sat up and threw her arms around his neck. "Yes, yes, I will, Alvin. I want to be your wife; b-but only on one condition," said Arielle.

"And what might that be?"

"Our first baby will be named Magic."

Alvin laughed out loud with happiness as he stood and swooped her up into his arms. "Of course, Arielle, of course. Thank you, darling, I'll prove my love to you every day of the year, every day of the month, every day of the week, every minute of the hour, every second of the minute and…."

Arielle put her fingers over his lips. "You're running out of time, my love."

Alvin laughed happily and Arielle's heart soared. "You can't possibly know how happy you've made me, Arielle."

Arielle looked at him lovingly and smiled. "As much as I don't want to, I have to tell Lucky Lady what happened. Will you come with me, Alvin?"

"Of course, I will."

Arielle and Alvin enter the aviary. "Hi, Lucky Lady," said Arielle.

"Hi, Miss Arielle, where's Magic?"

"He's gone, Lucky Lady, Magic's gone," said Arielle as tears start falling again.

"What do you mean?" asked Lucky Lady.

"He was killed when someone threw a stone at him,' said Arielle, crying.

"Oh, no, no, my Magic is gone?'

"Yes, Lucky Lady, he's gone but Magic was happy when he left because you and the children came back to him. That's what he wanted more than anything else in the world," said Alvin.

"Thank you, Alvin, for bringing us back here for Magic," said Lucky Lady.

"You're quite welcome. Oh, by the way, Lucky Lady, Miss Arielle has agreed to become my wife."

"Oh, my goodness, I'm so happy you'll be here with us, Alvin. I guess you could call this a bittersweet moment," said Lucky Lady.

"Yes, you sure can call it that, Lucky Lady," said Arielle sniffling.

Arielle and Alvin left and went into the big house to tell Ginger of their coming marriage.

"Good morning, Ginger," said Alvin.

"Well, good morning to you both. How are you feeling this morning, Arielle? I am so sorry to hear about Magic."

"I'm a little better, Ginger, thanks to Alvin. We're going to be married, Ginger, Alvin has just asked me to marry him." said Arielle.

Ginger jumped up and down. "Oh my heavens, I'm so happy for the two of you. When can we start planning the wedding?"

"As soon as we can," said Arielle.

"Yes, it can't be soon enough for me. I'm head over heels in love with this pretty lady, Ginger"

I'm glad, Alvin. It couldn't have come at a better time for Arielle. Where do you want to be married, Arielle?" asked Ginger.

Arielle looked at Alvin. "It doesn't matter, anywhere will be perfect," said Alvin.

"Let's make it under Old Noble, Ginger," said Arielle.

"All right, that's a perfect place. May I contact the queen to officiate at the wedding?"

"Sure, of course, I think she should be the one. Will you have her contact all the other fairies in the county and let them know too?" asked Arielle.

"I certainly will. I'll make all the preparations for the wedding including the decorations, Arielle, but I need to know a date," said Ginger.

"Thanks, Ginger, you're a sweetheart."

Arielle looked at Alvin again. "The sooner it is the better. I don't want to give her a chance to change her mind." Alvin looked at Arielle and winked.

"I would be a fool to do that, Alvin, I happen to be crazy in love with you," said Arielle smiling.

"Let's make it on Sunday, if the queen is available," said Alvin.

"All right, perfect. It'll give me a few days to get things in order," said Ginger.

Ginger contacted the queen to get her approval then prepareed for the wedding.

When Saturday arrived, Ginger is at Old Noble decorating. A white arch was placed near Old Noble for the scene of the wedding. Bluebells and white carnations with blue and white ribbons adorned it. White and silver garland hung on branches of Old Noble with pots of ferns hanging from limbs.

On Sunday Ginger is out early at Old Noble to set up the table. The cake is set in the middle of the table with a dazzling crystal amethyst set in the center. A bride and groom stood on each side of the amethyst. She placed a large green candle at each end of the table and tiny tulip buds are positioned all around. Tiny glasses are set out for a toast to the bride and groom with a bottle champagne.

On Sunday Queen Rhiannon arrived to officiate at the wedding then Arielle appeared in her breathtaking wedding gown.

When Alvin got there, Arielle looked at him and turned a rosy pink just thinking of becoming his wife. He winked at her and the services began.

Ginger remembered to bring the bubble machine with a small generator. When the ceremony was over, she started the bubble machine. A toast was given to the new bride and groom and the cake was cut. While everyone is eating and enjoying themselves, Arielle grabbed Alvin's hand and pulled him toward the bubble machine.

Arielle dragged him in front of the machine knowing that a bubble will surround them and carry them into space. They looked down at the crowd waving and smiling then they caress and kiss as the bubble drifted toward their penthouse. The bubble burst while they were over the penthouse. Alvin smiled at Arielle. "Perfect timing," he said.

As the days passed, Arielle settled into her new role as a housewife. She has less time to think about Magic now.

Several months have passed since the marriage. Arielle went to the aviary to see Lucky Lady and the children. She walked in and sat on the bench Alvin had placed in there for her. Lucky Lady flew over and perched on her shoulder.

"Hi, Lucky Lady, how have you been doing?"

"Better, much better."

"Good, I'm glad" Just as Arielle began to ask about the children, one of them flew up and landed on her other shoulder.

"Hi, Master," said the bird.

Arielle burst into tears of happiness and sorrow too, when memories flooded her mind. "Well, hello there," she said sniffling. "You are the spitting image of your father little one and you even sound like him. I could call you Magic, but there was only one of him, so I'm going to call you MJ for Magic, Jr.," said Arielle, wiping the tears from her eyes.

"Yeah, Master," said MJ. "Your father would be so proud of you, MJ" Arielle got up to leave with tears still glistening in her eyes.

"You come back, Miss Arielle?" asked Lucky Lady.

"Of course, and I won't wait so long the next time."

Alvin went to work in the villages every day to help the people plant shrubs and flowers. Each day when he got home, Arielle welcomed him with open arms.

"Hello there, sweet love of my life. You seem to be mighty happy today," said Alvin.

"Oh, yes, I am Alvin. I went down to see Lucky Lady and the children today. She is doing much better, and you won't believe what happened. One of the babies flew onto my shoulder. I named him MJ for Magic Jr."

"That's wonderful,"

"But the best part was when he landed on my shoulder he

said something that made me cry, not only for happiness but for
sorrow too."

"What did he say?"

"Hi, Master! Arielle burst into tears as she told Alvin about it.
He put his arms around her and held her close. "I'm glad you have
the babies and Lucky Lady. They're good for you."

"Thank you, Alvin, and I have you."

"Have I told you lately that you are the love of my life, forever
and ever?" he said.

Arielle looked at him and smiled. In turn, he winked and
kissed her.

During the next few months, Arielle spent a lot of time with
Lucky Lady and the children. She confided in Lucky Lady a lot as
she did with Magic. She still misses him so much. "Lucky Lady, I've
been mulling something over in my mind. I miss Magic terribly and
I want to honor him. He knew I was wrong, but he always obeyed
me with never a complaint," said Arielle.

"What are you thinking about, Miss Arielle?"

"I haven't discussed it with Alvin or Ginger yet but I'm thinking
about making the lower part of this mansion into a children's hospital
dedicating it to Magic's memory. What do you think, Lucky Lady?"

"Oh, Miss Arielle, Magic would be so honored and pleased to
know that you would do such a good thing in his memory."

"I'll talk it over with Alvin and Ginger and get back to you later."

"Okay, Miss Arielle."

When Alvin arrived home that evening, Arielle approached him
after supper.

"Alvin, I've been considering something and I want to know how
you feel about it."

"What is it, darling?"

"Well, if you agree, and I'll have to talk it over with Ginger too;
I would like to make the first two floors of this huge mansion into a
children's hospital honoring the memory of Magic."

"Ginger is part of our family and most of the responsibility would
rest on her so I'll have to get her approval too."

"I think it's a wonderful idea. I know how much you loved Magic. I say if it makes you feel better do it; absolutely, if Ginger is agreeable."

"Thank you, Alvin. Somehow I knew you wouldn't disagree. I'll talk to Ginger tomorrow."

The following morning, Arielle flew down to Ginger's to approach her with the idea. "Good morning, Ginger. I have something I want to discuss with you, but I want you to be very truthful because I don't want you feel obligated in any way."

"What is it, Arielle?"

"I've been mulling this over in my mind for months now. I would like to turn the two lower levels of this mansion into a children's hospital to honor Magic. Naturally, you'll reserve the third floor for yourself, but you would be the director with a huge responsibility. Would you want the job?"

Ginger looked at Arielle and a wide, warm smile formed across her lips.

"You have to ask me if I would want that job. Arielle? It would make me the happiest woman alive. A hospital for children in the name of Magic! What a wonderful thought and a beautiful gift of love and remembrance. Of course, I would be honored, Arielle."

Arielle flew up and kissed Ginger on the cheek. "Thank you, Ginger for being my friend." They both laughed happily.

Ginger stepped right into her new job ordering medical supplies, beds, television sets and rolling tables for eating in each room. Contacts were made to deliver the best equipment and other needed medical resources. Cooks and cleaning services were hired; then she sat down to design a sign for the hospital and approached Arielle when she finished.

When Ginger went to her apartment on the third floor, she said "I think I have everything covered, Arielle. I've designed the sign and I want to make sure you approve of it," said Ginger as she held the drawing up of the sign.

The design resembled a larger and longer version of a bonnet on a grandfather's clock. Perched at the top of the sign was a sculpted starling. Near the top it read, A Magic Wish and in large letters across the bottom was the name of the hospital; YE OLD NOBLE HOSPITAL FOR CHILDREN. Arielle looked at it and tears flowed down her cheeks again.

"It's beautiful, absolutely beautiful, Ginger, thank you so much. You are a precious jewel."

When word got out in all counties of the area of a new hospital for children, donations start pouring in. Letters of deep respect, that included money also, jam Ginger's mail box every day.

When Alvin returned home from Beaver Falls, Arielle met him at the door with a picture of the sign now under contract for the hospital, She looked at him blinking back the tears.

Alvin looked at it and shook his head. "Ginger is almost as amazing as you are, darling." He put his arms around her and kissed her tenderly.

"Now that everything is falling into place for the hospital, Alvin, could I go with you into the villages and help the people?"

"Of course! That will be wonderful but it's a long way out and back for you," said Alvin.

"Hmmm, what if I ask Lucky Lady if she would mind taking us out? The children are on their own now."

"That's an excellent idea. Why don't you ask her tomorrow?"

The next morning Arielle flew down to the aviary. "Good morning, Lucky Lady," said Arielle.

"Hi, Miss Arielle, what brings you here so early in the morning?"

"To ask a favor of you."

"Yes, and what might that be?"

"Would you consider taking Alvin and I to the villages to help the people?"

"Why, Miss Arielle, what an honor that would be. Of course, I'll be very happy to continue on with Magic's carpet rides," said Lucky Lady.

Arielle smiled and thought of the carpet rides with Magic. What a blessing it was for her to have him as long as she did. "Thank you, Lucky Lady. I'm so pleased to have you and the children."

The next day Arielle and Alvin flew down to the aviary for their trip to Beaver Falls. The village was peaceful. Their first stop had children and a mother working in their yard. Arielle approached the children and landed on Maggie's shoulder. "Good morning," said Arielle.

"Hey, Maggie, You have a fairy on your shoulder," yelled one of the children.

"Nuh-uh. No I don't. This isn't April Fool's Day Kaden. You're not even funny."

"Yes, you do, can't you see her?" asked Kaden. Maggie looked at one shoulder and then the other.

"Oh, golly, I do, don't I? How tiny she is."

Arielle laughed and it sounded like bells tinkling.

"She's beautiful! What's your name little fairy?" asked Maggie.

"My name is Arielle."

"That's a very pretty name, Arielle, did you come to play with us? asked Maggie.

"Oh yes, I surely did. What would you like to play?" asked Arielle.

"Ummm, I don't know," said Maggie.

"Well, let me think, how about blowing bubbles?" asked Arielle.

Maggie lowered her head. "But we don't have any bubbles," said Maggie sadly.

"I can fix that!" said Arielle.

With a wave of her wand hundreds of bubbles appeared and the children ran after them in glee. Arielle flew around the yard with her wand making bubbles by the hundreds. Alvin looked at her and smiled.

The children's mother watched the children chasing bubbles. "Where in the world did all the bubbles come from?" she asked.

"From my wife, Arielle and her magic wand. She's playing with the children."

"How nice of her." The mother smiled and continued her work. Alvin watched Arielle for a while getting a kick of her way with children. When it came time for Arielle to leave, the children are saddened.

"Will you come back to play with us again, Arielle?" asked Maggie.

"I certainly will, I had a lot of fun, didn't you?" asked Arielle.

"Yes, will you come back to play with me too?" asked April.

"Oh, yes, all of you. I had a very good time," said Arielle.

Maggie reminded Arielle of herself when she was little. She had been a little bashful and self-conscious. She relished every moment with the children. On the way home Alvin began a conversation.

"You were wonderful today with the children, darling. I loved to watch you romp in the grass with them."

"Little Maggie reminded me of myself when I was growing up.

"How's that?"

"Being bashful and self-conscious."

"I can't imagine you being self-conscious, Arielle. All the times I watched you, it looked as though you had plenty of confidence. But shy, yes, every time I looked your way, you turned a rosy pink and you still do."

"I know Alvin, and I hate it."

"No, no. Don't ever change. I love you all the more when you are a bright rosy pink" said Alvin smiling.

Arielle laughed and put her head on his shoulder and her arms around his waist until they arrived at the aviary.

"I had so much fun today, Alvin."

"I'm happy darling I loved to watch you play with the children." Alvin jumped off Lucky Lady and helped Arielle down and she stayed in the aviary with Lucky Lady until it was time for dinner.

"Thanks, Lucky Lady for taking us to the village today; I had such a wonderful time with the children."

"Yes, Miss Arielle, I watched you playing with the children, you looked very happy."

When Arielle left the aviary, she locked the gate and she flew to the penthouse. When she entered the house, Arielle plopped herself on the couch. "Oh, I'm tired those children wore me out today."

Alvin chuckled. "Too much for a little old lady, huh?" asked Alvin teasingly.

Arielle jumped up off the couch and reached into her pocket and pulled out her wand and aimed it at Alvin. He made a quick spin and he was standing in front of her in his black magic cloak.

Arielle let out a peal of laughter. "You asked for it Mister."

"Oh, I did, did I?"

"My but you look handsome in that cloak, Mister." teased Arielle.

"Don't try to butter me up Milady," said Alvin.

She gave him a zap and he held up his hand and beautiful red roses fell at her feet. She gave him another zap and he held up his hand up again and bubbles every color of the rainbow fill the room.

The zaps continue back and forth, sponge balls, rubber snakes, rubber spiders, rubber blocks and rubber duckies, you name it and they did it until they both fell onto the couch in tears because they're laughing so hard.

"I give, I give, I'm no match for you, Alvin," said Arielle laughing.

"Oh, on the contrary, darling, you're a perfect match," said Alvin as he put his arms around her and pulls her to him whispering something in her ear. She pushed him back laughing.

"Now, who's going to clean this mess up?" she asked Alvin.

"What mess?" asked Alvin.

"You're baaaad, Mr. Alvin."

"I know, Mrs. Alvin, and I love every minute of it," said Alvin as they both started gathering up the mess laughing all the while with their happiness.

The next day they went to the aviary to get Lucky Lady for their trip into Bay Village. The streets were quiet, Arielle was thankful for that. They flew until they found someone working in their yard.

"There, down there, Lucky Lady," yelled Arielle. She had spotted a man working in his garden. Lucky Lady whisked them down near the farmer and landed. Alvin and Arielle both flew onto a shoulder of the man.

"Good morning, sir;" said Alvin.

The gardener looked around but saw no one. We're here, sir, on your shoulders," said Arielle.

The gardener looked to the right and saw Arielle.

"Well, I'll be golly-darn if it isn't the prettiest little fairy I've ever laid eyes on," said the man.

"I agree, sir, she's my beautiful wife."

The gardener looked to the left on his other shoulder and there sat Alvin, a male fairy.

"This must be my lucky day," said the gardener.

"Why's that sir?" asked Alvin.

"Hardly anyone sees a fairy, but I'm seeing two in one day, unless I'm completely losing it," said the farmer shaking his head.

Alvin and Arielle both laugh and it sounded like large bells tinkling.

"No sir, you're not losing it. We like to visit the villagers to see what we can do to help," said Alvin.

"To help, eh?" asked the gardener.

"Yes sir. Is there anything we can do to help you or your family?" asked Arielle.

"Yeah? Well, maybe there is. Let's go to the house," said the farmer as he set his hoe aside.

"By the way, my name is Jim, and I'm very pleased to meet you both," he said.

Alvin and Arielle follow him into the house. He took them into a bedroom where his wife and a granddaughter were. Arielle and Alvin sat on each of the bed posts at the foot of the bed.

"Hello, are you both feeling all right?" asked Arielle.

"My goodness, what do we have here, Pa?" asked Jim's wife.

"It's a couple of little sprites," said Jim.

"Oh, no sir, we're not sprites, we're fairies," said Arielle.

"Where do you live?" asked the little girl.

"Near the forest and Old Noble," answered Arielle.

"Oh, I've heard of Old Noble. That's an old oak hundreds of years old," said the girl.

"That's right. The fairies gather there quite often for meetings, and weddings too," said Arielle.

"That is right. The fairies gather quite often for meetings and I might add, weddings too," said Alvin as he glanced over at Arielle giving her a wink.

"They do? Can I come see them some time?"

"Of course you can, but they're not there every day. We would have to let you know when they'll be there," said Alvin.

"Can you, would you?"

"Now, Honor how could you manage that?" asked Jim, her grandfather.

Honor hung her head and tears fell down her cheeks. Arielle and Alvin looked at each other with questioning eyes.

"I know Grandpapa, but maybe they can make me well. I've heard that fairies are magic; Grandmama, maybe they can make you well too," said Honor with tears streaming down her face.

The desperation of Honor tugged at the hearts of both Alvin and Arielle.

"Now, not to worry, my beautiful wife is almost ready to open a hospital for children; perhaps you can be our first patient, Honor. We'll have doctors and nurses that can also help your grandmother," said Alvin with concern in his voice.

"Well, I'll be a monkey's uncle, this is my lucky day doubled," said Jim.

Alvin and Arielle smiled.

"My friend, Ginger, is the director of the hospital. As soon as she lets me know when they're having the opening day, we'll fly out and tell you and, if necessary, we can have you picked up for the opening," said Arielle.

"Thank you, thank you so much. We want our precious granddaughter to get well so she can live a happy and normal life. Bless you, my children," said the gardener's wife.

Jim left the room and Alvin and Arielle followed.

"I don't know what made you stop here, but I do know that you have made my wife and I the happiest people this side of the world with hopes of curing our beautiful granddaughter," said Jim.

"Hope rests in the soul of each and every one of us, sir. Never give up," said Alvin smiling.

When Alvin and Arielle got home, they sat on the bench outside.

"I wonder what's wrong with Honor," said Arielle.

"I don't know, but I hope the doctors will be able to cure her. That would be a miracle for Magic, wouldn't it darling?"

Arielle looked at Alvin and smiled then reached over and took his hand.

"Yes, it truly would be. Magic's first miracle. I can't imagine having a child with a handicap that couldn't be cured," said Arielle as she raised his hand to her lips and kissed it tenderly.

"You are a very special person, Arielle."

Arielle smiled, it made her feel very good inside.

"Thanks, Alvin. Only because of you. I need all the support I can get."

The next day Arielle went to see Ginger to check on the status of the grand opening of the hospital.

"Hi, Ginger, how are things going at the hospital?"

"Just a couple of loose ends to be tied up and we'll be ready."

"Good, will you do me a favor?" asked Arielle.

"Sure, you know I will. What is it?"

"Contact Queen Rhiannon and have her call a special meeting under Old Noble on Sunday," said Arielle knowing what she had to do during that meeting.

"Sure, I'll do that," said Ginger.

On Sunday, Arielle and Alvin flew out to Old Noble. Arielle wanted Alvin to hear what she had to say. Queen Rhiannon and all the fairies from the county have gathered under Old Noble.

Arielle walked up to the make-shift stage and began her speech,

"Thanks for coming everyone. I want you to know our hospital will have its grand opening on Tuesday and you are all invited. This hospital has been made possible by the people in the villages and was built in the memory of my friend, Magic."

Arielle started to tear up She looked around the crowd and spotted Clover and Naida. Ginger walked up close to the stage to relieve her for a moment.

"Hi, I'll take over until Arielle gains her composure. I've been selected by Arielle to be the director of the hospital. We've hired children's specialists for doctors and nurses. We have a room to treat adults if necessary. No one will be turned away," said Ginger as she looked at Arielle.

Arielle nodded her head and returned to the stage. "I want to apologize to everyone in the villages that I have offended and especially, you, Queen Rhiannon, Clover and Naida but also to all the fairies that I have shown disrespect toward our sacred covenants. I sincerely hope you will find it in your hearts to forgive me," said Arielle as her voice breaks. "Ginger will complete the meeting now." Thanks everyone for being here," said Arielle as she stepped aside for Ginger to complete the meeting.

Alvin stood by listening to Arielle's apology with a big lump in his throat. He realized what a difficult decision she had made to admit her wrongdoing. He was surprised but very proud.

"To all of you, we invite your presence in the hospital to cheer sick children. You may help with a miracle cure more than you realize just by allowing the child to see and believe in fairies and miracles," said Ginger smiling.

The meeting adjourned and everyone went home.

Later, Alvin approached Arielle.

"I was so proud of you today, darling. It took a lot of courage to admit your wrongdoing before everyone," he said.

"I had to do it, Alvin. It was preying on my mind and I couldn't let it interfere with any decisions I make regarding the hospital."

Alvin took her into his arms and held her close. The following day, Alvin and Arielle went to Lucky Lady in the aviary and flew to Bay Village to see Honor and her grandparents.

Alvin approached Jim in the yard "Hello, sir. How are you and your family today?" asked Alvin.

"About the same, I'd say," said Jim.

"We want you to know that the hospital will be open on Tuesday. Will you need anyone to pick up Honor and your wife," asked Alvin.

"No sir. I can manage to bring them in. Thank you sir from

the bottom of my heart, I shall never forget the caring and kindness shown by both of you," said Jim.

"You're very welcome sir and we'll look forward to that little granddaughter of yours to be on the road to recovery along with your wife," said Alvin.

After their trip, Alvin and Arielle flew onto Lucky Lady and returned to their penthouse.

"I'm so excited about the hospital, Alvin. I want it to be a huge success."

"And it will be, darling, it certainly will be."

"I've been so happy since we've been married, Alvin. I sometimes think back about the times I was so terrible," said Arielle.

"And?" asked Alvin.

"When I thought you were a wacko," said Arielle.

"A what?"

"And a creep," said Arielle.

"A what?"

"And an oddball," said Arielle.

"A what?"

"And almost a chipmunk!"

"A what?"

"And I was going to fly you to the moon in a cocoon," said Arielle laughing,

"You what?"

Arielle started running away from him knowing he was going to chase her.

Alvin caught her and threw her down on the floor tickling her until she gave up.

"I give, I give. I did, Alvin, I really did, but I know different now. You are the best thing that ever happened to me. You are my life, my love, and my everything and I love you so very much," said Arielle catching her breath.

"I certainly hope so because you're not ever, ever going to get rid of me," said Alvin smiling at her.

Arielle reached up and pulled him toward her and they lay there laughing and looking up at the sky.

In the morning, Arielle went down to see Lucky Lady and the children in the aviary.

"Hi, Miss Arielle," said Lucky Lady.

"Hi, how's everyone doing?" asked Arielle.

"We're doing just fine. How's the hospital coming along?"

"The grand opening is tomorrow. I'm very excited, Lucky Lady."

"I'll bet you are."

"Not only about the hospital though," said Arielle smiling.

"What else could you possibly be excited about... Unless?"

"Yes, yes, its true Lucky Lady, we are with baby" said Arielle.

Lucky lady screamed and flew around the aviary doing flips just as Magic had done. Arielle sat there watching her memories play out before her eyes and she started crying.

"Why the tears Miss Arielle?" asked Lucky Lady.

"I just saw Magic in you, plus I'm so happy anyway... just an emotional minute, Lucky Lady. I haven't said anything to Alvin yet about the baby. I'm waiting for that special moment."

"Yes, yes, yes, I'm so happy for you both. You are a very lucky lady and, Miss Arielle, there is no special moment; any moment is special," said Lucky Lady.

"Okay, Lucky Lady, thanks, I'll remember that."

Arielle smiled, shook her head in disbelief and waved as she stepped out the door.

"Don't forget Miss Arielle, any moment is special."

Arielle looked back. "Thank you Lucky Lady," she shut the door and locked it then flew to the penthouse.

When Alvin arrived home that evening Arielle is sitting on the couch. "Alvin, come sit here by me," said Arielle as she patted the couch next to her.

"What's going on, darling is something wrong with Lucky Lady or Ginger or one of the babies? You're not sick are you?"

Arielle giggled. "No, of course not, they're all fine and I'm fine but speaking of babies, Alvin, we are with baby."

Alvin's eyes popped wide open with happiness shining through.

"We are? A baby? Whoopee! He jumped up and swept Arielle up and circled around the penthouse. Oh, golly, golly, I'm so happy. We're going to have a little baby Magic.

Arielle laughed happily watching his reaction. "That sounds too funny, Alvin, a little baby Magic," said Arielle laughing.

"Tell Ginger tomorrow, tell Ginger! She'll be so happy, said Alvin.

Arielle flew down to the mansion the next morning to tell Ginger the news of the baby.

"Ginger, I have good news. We're going to have a baby," said Arielle smiling Ginger started dancing and screaming around the room.

"A baby, a baby, oh, Arielle, I can't wait. If I could hug you, I would but I'm afraid I'd squish you I'm so happy. What are we going to name her, uh, him?"

"Its name will be Magic, whether it's a boy or girl."

"Magic," I like that, Arielle, I like it," said Ginger smiling happily.

The next six months both women are busy making clothes and things for the baby. Ginger made bassinet for the baby's bed out of twigs she had collected in the forest. She used a beautiful lace eyelet and sewed silk tulip buds in place around the hood. When Arielle saw the bassinet, she's ecstatic.

"Ginger, it's beautiful, I love it, but you have to slow down. You're trying to do too much for the baby and working at the hospital too."

Alvin happens to walk in at that time hearing what Arielle said.

"Yes, she's right Ginger. We don't want you getting sick. We still have plenty of time before the baby gets here," said Alvin.

"Okay, okay, I don't need two of you picking on me. I'll slow down... hut just for a few minutes."

They laughed; Alvin shook his head and Arielle flew up to give her a kiss on the cheek. "Don't mind my fat little body, Ginger, it just takes me a little longer to get where I want to go."

They all laugh happily again.

Honor is admitted to the hospital and the doctors are running tests to find the problem she's having. A doctor has seen her grandmother and put her on medication and she's doing well.

Fairies are coming into the hospital every day to entertain the children. The ones that are coming by the most often are Queen Rhiannon, Clover and Naida according to Ginger.

Arielle stopped by to see how Ginger is doing the following week.

"Arielle, what brings you here? Is everything all right?"

"Oh yes, Ginger. I just wanted to make sure everything is going all right for you."

"Are there are any problems with the hospital?"

"Well, not exactly with the hospital."

"What do you mean?"

"One of the interns keeps coming around bugging me."

"Bugging you?"

"Yeah, I can't get any work done when he's hanging around."

"Why, Ginger!" said Arielle.

"What?"

"It sounds like you may have a suitor," said Arielle giggling.

Ginger looked at Arielle and laughed loudly. "Are you joking?"

"No madam, I'm not, I just went through the same thing about a year ago. Remember, Ginger?"

Ginger laughed again. "I don't have time for a suitor, Arielle," said Ginger.

"Well now, we'll just have to make time, won't we?"

"What do you mean by that?"

"Nothing, Ginger, nothing at all. I'll see you later," said Arielle.

Ginger shook her head and smiled. She knew what Arielle meant.

"Okay, Arielle, take care." Ginger smiled again and carried on with her business.

Arielle prepared supper then sat on the couch thinking.

"You're very quiet tonight, Arielle is something wrong?" asked Alvin.

"No, not really. Just thinking."

"Thinking about what?"

"Nothing".

Alvin looked at her and she looked at him and smiled.

"Come on, out with it. I see those little cogs on the wheel turning in that pretty little head of yours. Spit it out, darling"

"I'm trying to figure out a way to get Ginger and an intern together. He's hanging around her just like you were hanging around me."

Alvin laughed. "So, cupid, you think you have it all figured out, huh?"

"I don't know, but I'd like to think so," said Arielle,

"Well now, since the hospital is new and it has been such a success, why wouldn't she want to throw a party?"

Arielle looked at him with big and surprised eyes. "Alvin, you're a genius and a sweetheart. Thank you, love, but where should it be held?"

"Her place, of course," said Alvin.

Arielle looked at him and gave him a devilish grin. "And you men think women are devious?"

Alvin roared with laughter.

A few months before Arielle is expecting the baby, Ginger started preparing for the baby shower. She called on Clover and Naida to help, but soon afterwards Arielle approached Ginger.

"Ginger, the six month anniversary for the hospital is coming up and I want a party thrown for the staff of doctor's after hours on Friday. Several of us have arranged everything so you won't have to lift a finger," said Arielle.

"Golly, Arielle, that's very nice of you. Where will it be?"

"At your place."

"At my place?"

"Did I hear an echo?

Ginger laughed. "I guess you did. All right, Arielle, at my place, Friday night. I'll let the staff of doctor's know."

"Super," said Arielle.

Early Friday afternoon the caterers arrive at Ginger's home on the third floor of the hospital. They began setting up tables and chairs. The foods were kept hot in the ovens.

Wines and champagne were generously placed around the tables. A team of decorators came and decorated the house lavishly. Beautiful music is playing in the background.

When Ginger got off work, she went upstairs and opened the door and received the surprise of her life. Everything looked and smelled so beautiful.

"Oh my goodness! Am I in the right place?" asked Ginger teasingly.

The caterers and decorators look at her and laughed. She couldn't believe her eyes. They had done such a beautiful job of decorating.

While everyone was taking care of their job, Ginger stepped into her bedroom and locked the door, showered and dressed for the evening. While dressing, she heard a tiny little knock on the window. She looked over and saw Arielle. She went to the window and opened it.

"Hi, Ginger, how beautiful you are."

Ginger blushed. "Thanks Arielle, you guys went a little far out didn't you?"

"We're always far out, Ginger, haven't you learned that yet? Here, let me add a little something."

Arielle waved her wand and wound Ginger's hair up on top of her head. She waved it again and there were fresh bluebells peeking out from under her curls.

"Oh, Arielle, it's so beautiful," said Ginger while looking in the mirror.

Arielle stood back and looked at Ginger. "Hmmm, something is missing, ah, yes!" said Arielle. She circled her wand and a beautiful diamond necklace encircled Ginger's neck.

"Arielle, no, this is too much!"

"No, milady, it's perfect!"

"No, no, Arielle, I'm not used to dressing like this, it's t-too beautiful," said Ginger.

"Just as you are, milady. Oh, Oh! I hear the doorbell, I'll see you later," whispered Arielle.

Arielle disappeared from the window before Ginger could say

anything more. When Ginger went to the door, she opened it and Dr. Eric Mitchell stood before her, the intern that had been bugging her.

"Well, good evening beautiful lady!" said Dr. Mitchell.

Ginger blushed. "Hi, Dr. Mitchell, come in," said Ginger.

He looked very handsome dressed in a suit rather than hospital garb, Ginger thought.

"You look very lovely tonight, Miss Lamont," said Dr. Mitchell.

"Thank you and you may call me Ginger, Dr. Mitchell."

"Well then, please call me Eric," said Dr. Mitchell.

The doorbell kept ringing during the evening and soon the condo was filled with doctors, both men and women having a good time.

Ginger decided she wasn't going to mention anything about the hospital; after all, this was a celebration. She and Dr. Mitchell stood by watching everyone while talking and she looked up at him.

"You look much different in clothes, Eric," said Ginger.

When she realized what she had said she turned beet red. Eric roared with laughter and looked at her. "Why, Miss Ginger, you're blushing."

"Y-Yes, what I meant to say is you looked much different in a suit than in hospital garb. I-I'm sorry," said Ginger.

Eric smiled and took Ginger's hand. "I understand. Please, I'd like to dance with you," he said as he led her to the living room dance floor.

"All right, b-but I'm not very good at dancing," said Ginger.

"Nor am I," replied Eric.

Ginger smiled as they floated across the floor. She felt beautiful while she seemed to stay in step with him.

Arielle couldn't stand it any longer; she had to take a peek at what was happening. She slipped out and flew around to a window. She saw Ginger dancing with a very handsome man and she appeared to be enjoying it. She hoped it was the intern.

Ginger glanced over and saw Arielle and waved her away; then she nodded her head yes, letting Arielle know it was the intern. Arielle flew around happily then flew to the penthouse smiling gleefully.

Ginger was disappointed when the evening was over. She felt like

Cinderella that was about to lose her glass slipper. "I've really enjoyed the evening with you, Eric. It has been such fun," said Ginger.

"And I have with you also, lovely lady. It's too bad the evening went by so fast. Perhaps we can go out another evening, Ginger," said Eric.

"Yes, I would like that."

"May I call on you then?"

"Yes, I'd like that too."

After the clean-up and everyone was gone, it was lonely and Ginger started thinking about Eric. She was glad Arielle had planned the party. She looked forward to seeing him at work tomorrow. Maybe he wasn't such a pain after all. She liked him.

Ginger was awakened in the early morning with a frantic knock on her window.

"Ginger, Ginger, come quick, Arielle's having the baby," called out Alvin excitedly.

Ginger grabbed her robe and hurried up to the penthouse. By the time she got there, the baby was born. Alvin bundled him up and took him to the living room for Ginger to see. Arielle went over and sat on the bench.

"Oh, my goodness, he's so tiny; he's no bigger than a thimble. Is he big enough to live, Arielle?"

Arielle laughed, "Of course he is Ginger, he's a fairy. We're all tiny. He's so adorable isn't he Ginger. He looks like Alvin doesn't he?"

"Yes, he does, he surely does," said Ginger lovingly.

Alvin was so proud he was beaming.

Ginger didn't go to work the next day. After being up all night, she was tired and wanted to stay close to Arielle if she needed her for anything.

Later in the day someone knocked at her door. When she opened it, Eric was standing before her and her heart started beating rapidly.

"I'm sorry to bother you, Ginger, I missed you at work and thought there might be something wrong," said Eric.

Ginger smiled. "No, there isn't anything wrong, everything is just right. I was called out during the night. My best friend had a baby boy. Come in, Eric."

Ginger ushered him to the sofa. "Wonderful, thanks. Now tell me more about the baby."

Ginger is nervous. She'd made such a fool out of herself last night. "May I get you something to drink, Eric?"

"Sure, thanks. I'll have a cup of coffee if you have any made."

"I sure do."

After she brought in the coffee, she sat next to him.

"Now, how about the baby?" asked Eric.

"Oh, yes, a beautiful baby boy."

"And his name?" asked Eric.

"Magic," said Ginger.

"That's an unusual name," said Eric.

"Yes, it is Eric, but these are unusual people."

"What do you mean?"

"Do you believe in fairies, Eric?"

"Well, I've never seen one, but I guess I do."

"I met Arielle one day while I was working in my garden. She had been sleeping on a bed of ferns when I disturbed her. Arielle is the founder of this hospital and everything good in it," said Ginger.

"I'd love to meet her, Ginger."

"Yes, I'll arrange for you to meet the whole family, but if you look closely while you're in the hospital, you'll find fairy folk everywhere around the children; especially around children."

Alan listened intently. He wasn't sure he believed in fairies but he was open to the idea. "You're a very interesting person, Ginger. Well, I guess I'd better leave now, thanks for the coffee. I think I'll stop by the hospital and look for some of those fairy folk."

Ginger smiled and walked him to the door. "Thanks for stopping by, Eric."

"It's my pleasure. When may I see you again, Ginger? Tonight, I hope?"

Ginger smiled. "I'd like that, Eric. Why don't you come back for dinner this evening. I'll invite Arielle and the family over so you can meet them.

"Great, it sounds wonderful….and the time?"

"Oh yes, six o'clock will be fine."

"All right, I'll see you this evening lovely lady." Eric bent over and kissed her on the cheek. She blushed while feelings that she's never known before pulsates throughout her body. After he left, Ginger rushed up to the penthouse.

"Arielle, come here for a minute," said Ginger excitedly.

"What is it, Ginger?"

"Eric is coming over for dinner tonight and I'd like for all of you to meet him. He's wonderful Arielle; I think I'm falling in love."

Arielle dances around and around. "I love it, I love it. Oh, Ginger, I'm so happy for you. Yes, yes, we'll be over. Thank you."

At six o'clock Eric arrived. Ginger has dinner ready and they sat down to eat. She had set a small table on a card table to accommodate Alvin and Arielle. The baby was placed in his bassinet near the table.

I went back to the hospital today, Ginger, and you're absolutely right; there were fairy folk all around the children. It was unbelievable. I don't know why I didn't notice them before," said Eric.

"Most people don't, Eric. Their minds are absorbed with too many other things," said Ginger.

"Oh, by the way, I found what the problem is with Honor. She'll have to have surgery to correct it but she'll be fine." said Alan.

"Eric, that's absolutely wonderful, I can't wait to tell Arielle and Alvin. I'm very proud of you. One day you'll be the best of the best."

"Ginger, you're an extraordinary person, and a beautiful one at that."

Ginger smiled and blushed while her emotions churn inside. At seven o'clock. Arielle and the family arrive to meet Alan.

"Arielle, Alvin, I'd like you to meet Dr. Eric. He works as an intern at the hospital."

"I'm very pleased to meet the both of you and your new baby, Magic. Ginger has told me so much about you and she has introduced to me to fairy life"

"We're very pleased to meet you too, Dr. Eric," said Alvin.

Eric and Ginger both held the baby in their hand. "He is the tiniest baby I've ever seen," said Eric. "It's hard to believe something this small could have life."

"There are other things smaller than he is," said Arielle. "Even an ant is smaller than him." she said laughing.

You are right you know. We have an awesome creator when you think about it," said Alvin.

"That's very true," said Eric. "I never thought of it that way. I don't know that I'd ever want to try surgery on one this small. He's smaller than my little finger. I'd have to use tweezers." Everyone roared with laughter.

Hopefully, he'll be a happy, healthy little boy that won't require surgery, said Ginger.

The evening went by wonderfully. Alvin and Arielle left for the penthouse and soon it was time for Alan to leave also. Ginger walked him to the door and he took her into his arms and kissed her goodnight.

"I'll see you at the hospital tomorrow, Ginger, good night pretty lady."

Ginger didn't sleep that night thinking of Eric. She felt warm and fuzzy all over and in disbelief.

Months have passed. Eric and Ginger have fallen in love. One evening after Eric got off work, he ran up to Ginger's apartment and knocked on the door. Ginger opened it and Eric dropped on one knee with a bouquet of red roses. "Ginger, I love you more than anything else in the world, will you marry me? Will you be my wife?"

Ginger turned rosy red. "Yes Alvin, oh yes I will, I will, but will you please get up off the floor?"

Alan laughed and got up and took her into his arms and kissed her tenderly. They were married under Old Noble, a tradition that began with Arielle and one Ginger never wants to be broken.

One evening Arielle and Alvin are sitting on their bench outside while the baby is sitting on the floor of the penthouse playing with a car Alvin had made him. A fly buzzed around the baby and he waved it off with his hand but the fly was persistent and came again. Magic looked at the fly and held out a finger and zapped it and the fly fell to the ground.

Arielle and Alvin looked at each other and giggled. "Well, we certainly didn't have to wait long to find out that Magic has it in him too, said Arielle."

"You're certainly right, darling. He didn't stand a chance did he? I guess he got the zap instead of the cloak but at least he looks like me." They both roared with joyous laughter.

Suddenly, a bolt of lightning struck and lit up the penthouse grounds. Arielle glanced up and saw starlings migrating to the south. A feather floated down and landed in her lap and she picked it up and looked back up to the sky.

"Thank you Magic, a change will come in a flash you said, and indeed it did," said Arielle.